My Little Book of
SPACE

by Peter Grego

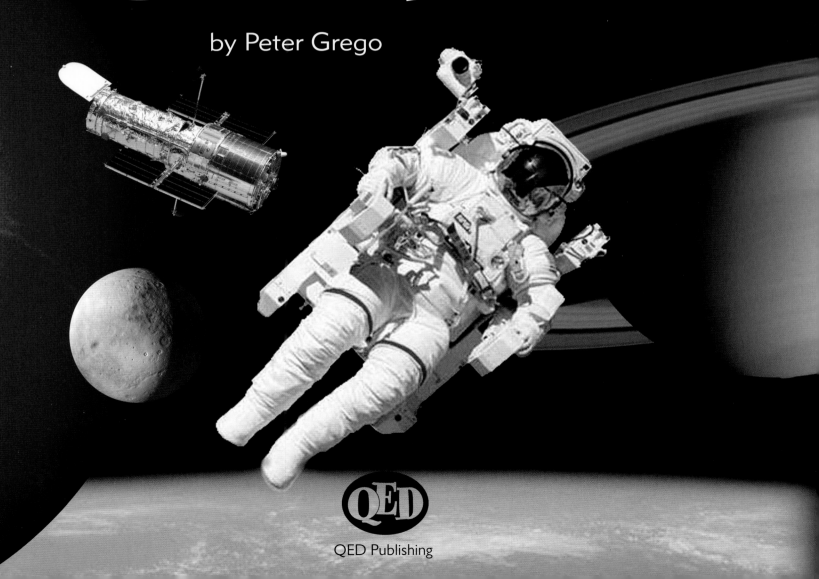

QED
QED Publishing

Copyright © QED Publishing 2014

Design: Starry Dog Books Ltd
Editor: Ruth Symons

First published in the UK in 2014 by
QED Publishing
A Quarto Group company
The Old Brewery
6 Blundell Street
London N7 9BH

www.qed-publishing.co.uk

A catalogue record for this book is
available from the British Library.

ISBN 978 1 78171 555 0

Printed in China

Words in **bold** are
explained in the
glossary on page 60.

Contents

Solar System

The Solar System is made up of the Sun and all the objects that circle, or **orbit**, around it. These include the planets and their moons.

Sun

Venus

Mars

Mercury

Earth

« The Sun is a bright star at the centre of the Solar System.

Jupiter

There are eight planets in the Solar System, including the Earth. Thousands of rocks, or asteroids, and millions of icy chunks, known as comets, also travel around the Sun.

Uranus

Neptune

Saturn

5

The Sun

The Sun is a ball of hot, bright, burning gas. It is the nearest star to the Earth.

>> The Sun is so big that a million Earths could fit inside it.

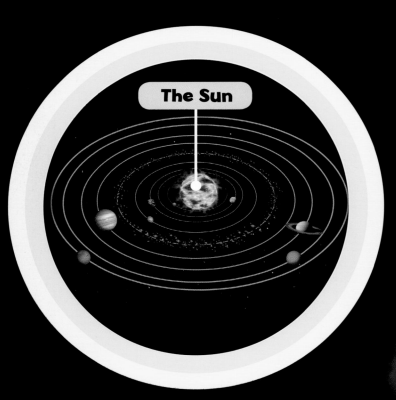

The Sun

⌃ The planets circle, or orbit, the Sun.

You should never look straight at the Sun. It is so bright that it can damage your eyes.

˅ **The Sun provides the Earth with light and warmth.**

Mercury

Mercury is the planet nearest to the Sun. It is the smallest planet in the Solar System.

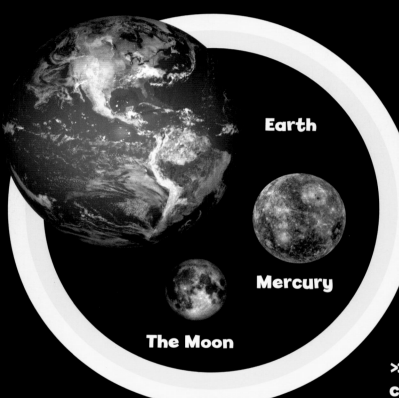

Earth

Mercury

The Moon

⌃ **Mercury is only a little bigger than the Earth's Moon.**

≫ **Mercury is covered with** craters. **These were made by** meteorites **and asteroids hitting the planet.**

Like the Earth, Mercury has a hard surface, but it has no **atmosphere**. No wind ever blows there, and clouds never drift across its skies.

⌄ **This crater on Mercury looks as if it has a smiley face!**

9

Venus

Venus is the second planet from the Sun. It is the hottest planet in the Solar System.

˅ **Venus is about the same size as the Earth.**

Venus

Sun

˄ **Venus can often be seen as a bright point of light after sunset or before sunrise.**

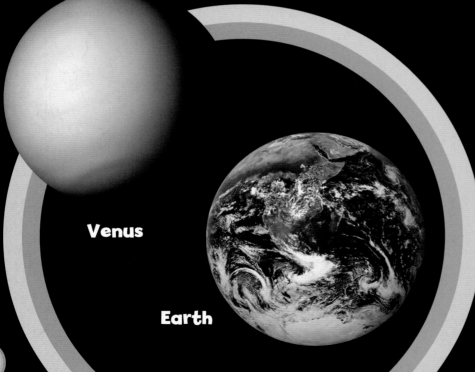

Venus

Earth

Venus is surrounded by thick clouds of poisonous gases. Beneath these, the rocky planet is covered with high mountains and deep valleys.

▼ This is what Venus looks like beneath its thick atmosphere.

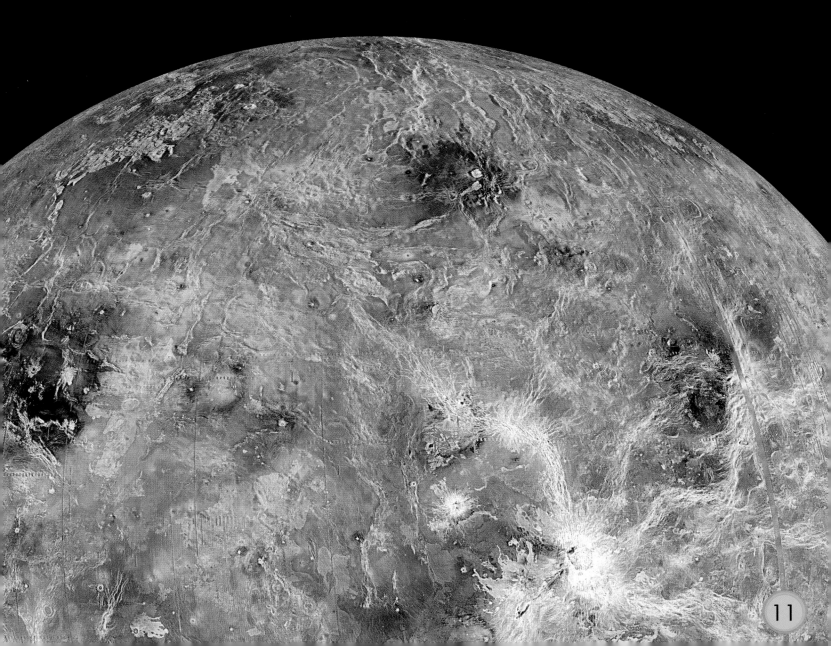

The Earth

The Earth is the third planet from the Sun. It is the only planet where we know life exists.

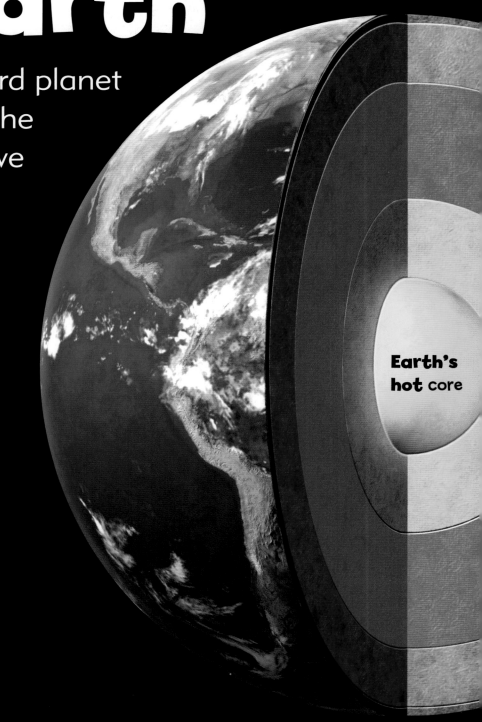

>> **The Earth is hot on the inside but cool on the surface.**

Earth's hot core

The Earth is a rocky planet covered by dry land, deep oceans and frozen **ice caps**. It is surrounded by a layer of air, called the atmosphere.

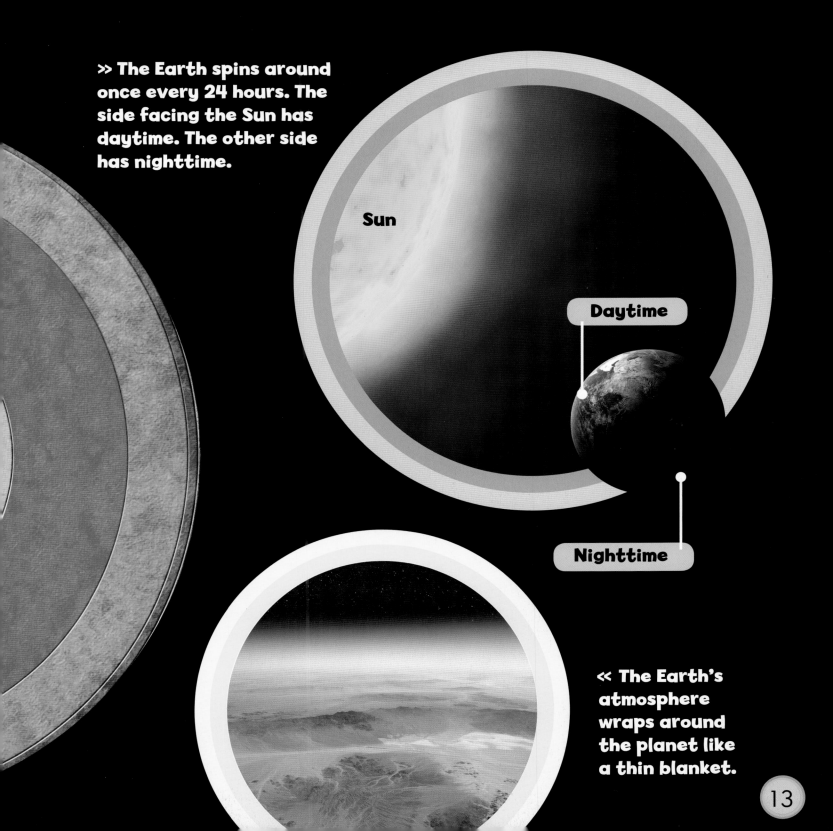

>> The Earth spins around once every 24 hours. The side facing the Sun has daytime. The other side has nighttime.

Sun

Daytime

Nighttime

<< The Earth's atmosphere wraps around the planet like a thin blanket.

The Moon

The Moon is a rocky ball about a quarter of the Earth's size. It circles the Earth once every 28 days.

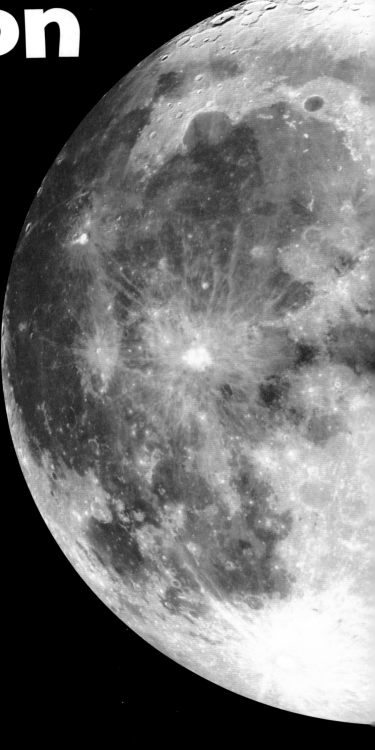

⌄ **There is no weather on the Moon. It is never cloudy or wet there.**

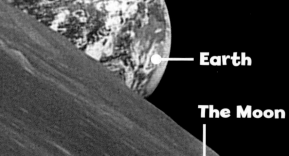

Earth

The Moon

>> This phase is called a crescent moon.

We can only see the part of the Moon that reflects the Sun's light. As the Moon circles the Earth, it looks like it is changing shape. The shapes are called phases.

⌃ Parts of the Moon are covered with dark 'seas' where lava once flowed.

15

Mars

Mars is a rocky, red planet about half the size of the Earth. It is the fourth planet from the Sun.

⋎ **Mars has lots of volcanoes. One of them, Olympus Mons, is the biggest volcano in the Solar System.**

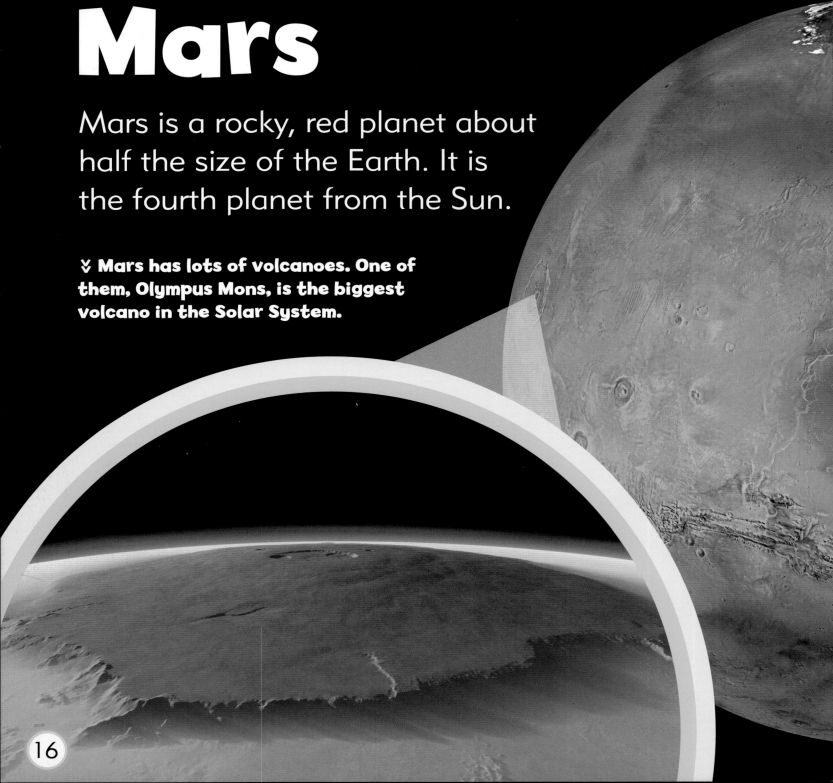

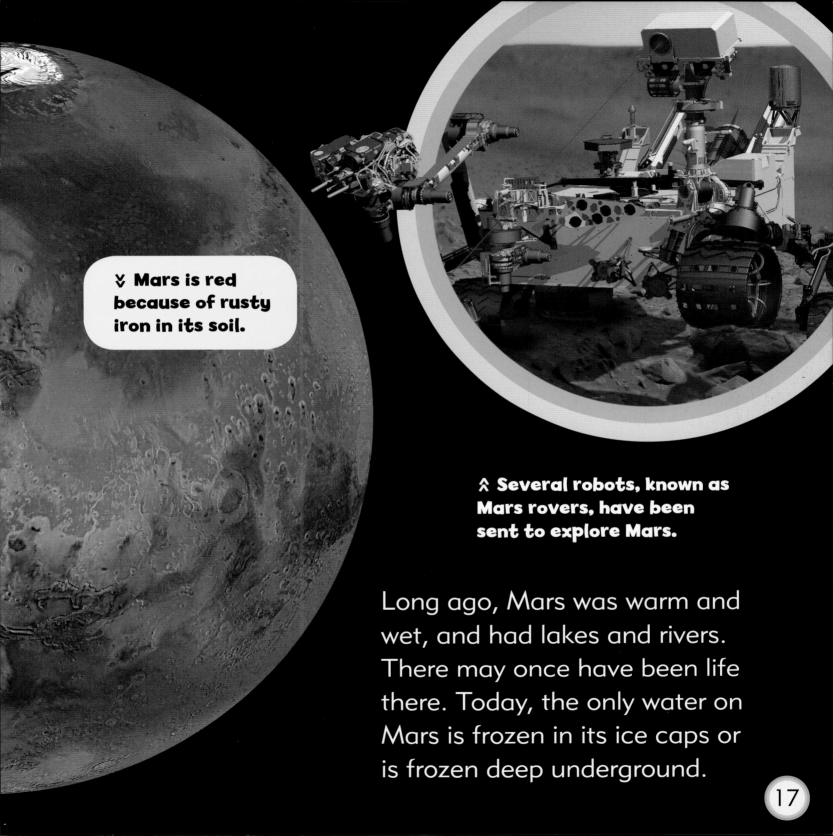

⩗ Mars is red because of rusty iron in its soil.

⩘ Several robots, known as Mars rovers, have been sent to explore Mars.

Long ago, Mars was warm and wet, and had lakes and rivers. There may once have been life there. Today, the only water on Mars is frozen in its ice caps or is frozen deep underground.

Jupiter

Jupiter is the fifth planet from the Sun and the biggest planet in the Solar System.

Io

Europa

Ganymede

Callisto

« Jupiter has more than 63 moons. The biggest moons are labelled here.

>> The Great Red Spot is a huge storm in Jupiter's atmosphere.

<< You could fit 1321 Earths inside Jupiter!

Jupiter is a **gas giant** with no solid surface. Its swirling bands of cloud and many storms make it a very colourful planet.

Saturn

Saturn is the sixth planet from the Sun. It is surrounded by wide rings, and has more than 60 moons. Its biggest moon is called Titan.

⌃ **Saturn is the second-largest planet in the Solar System.**

≪ Titan is covered with lakes, rivers and seas. These are made of liquid methane, **not water.**

Saturn is a gas giant with a small, rocky core. This huge planet takes 30 years to travel around the Sun.

≫ **Saturn's rings are made from millions of lumps of ice.**

Uranus

Uranus is the seventh planet from the Sun. It takes Uranus 84 years to travel once around the Sun.

⌄ Uranus has a set of very faint rings.

« Uranus has 27 moons. Most of them are made of ice and rock.

— Uranus

Puck

Miranda

Ariel

Umbriel

Titania

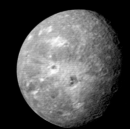
Oberon

Miranda

⌃ **Uranus' moon Miranda is covered with craters, grooves and cliffs.**

Uranus is a gas giant four times bigger than the Earth. It is so far away and faint that it was only discovered in 1781.

Neptune

Neptune is the farthest planet from the Sun. It takes Neptune 165 years to travel around the Sun.

⌄ **Streaky white clouds appear bright against the planet's blue colour.**

>> The huge, dark area is a storm in Neptune's atmosphere.

↗ **Neptune's biggest moon, Triton, is covered with ice volcanoes.**

Neptune is a gas giant nearly four times the size of the Earth. It has the strongest winds in the Solar System. Sometimes dark storms or clouds appear on Neptune.

Dwarf planets

The dwarf planets are smaller than the main planets. Most of them are made of ice.

>> Pluto was once called a planet, but it was renamed a dwarf planet in 2006.

Eris

Haumea

Makemake

Ceres

<< Four of the dwarf planets are shown here.

Ceres is found between Mars and Jupiter. All the other dwarf planets are found far beyond Neptune, in a zone called the Kuiper Belt.

⌄ **The Kuiper Belt is made up of millions of icy and rocky objects that orbit the Sun.**

Comets

Comets are city-sized chunks of ice and dirt. They move around the Sun following egg-shaped paths.

⌄ **Most comets come from the Oort Cloud. This is a zone halfway between the Sun and our next nearest star.**

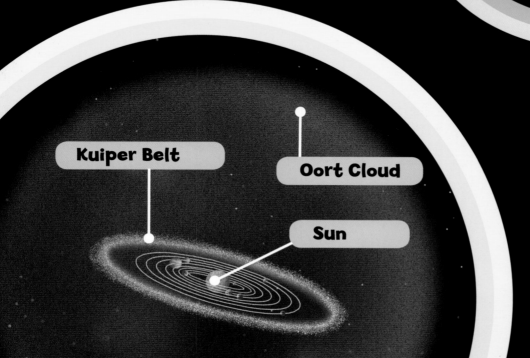

Kuiper Belt

Oort Cloud

Sun

⌃ **Halley's Comet, named after astronomer Edmond Halley, appears every 76 years.**

As comets approach the Sun, they start to melt and give off gas and dust. Glowing in the sunlight, the gas and dust make long, bright tails.

« At the centre of a comet is a huge, icy ball of dirt.

Earth

Asteroids

Asteroids are lumps of rock that orbit the Sun. Sometimes they hit planets and make craters.

⌃ Eros is an asteroid about the size of a city.

« An asteroid hit the Earth 65 million years ago and wiped out the dinosaurs.

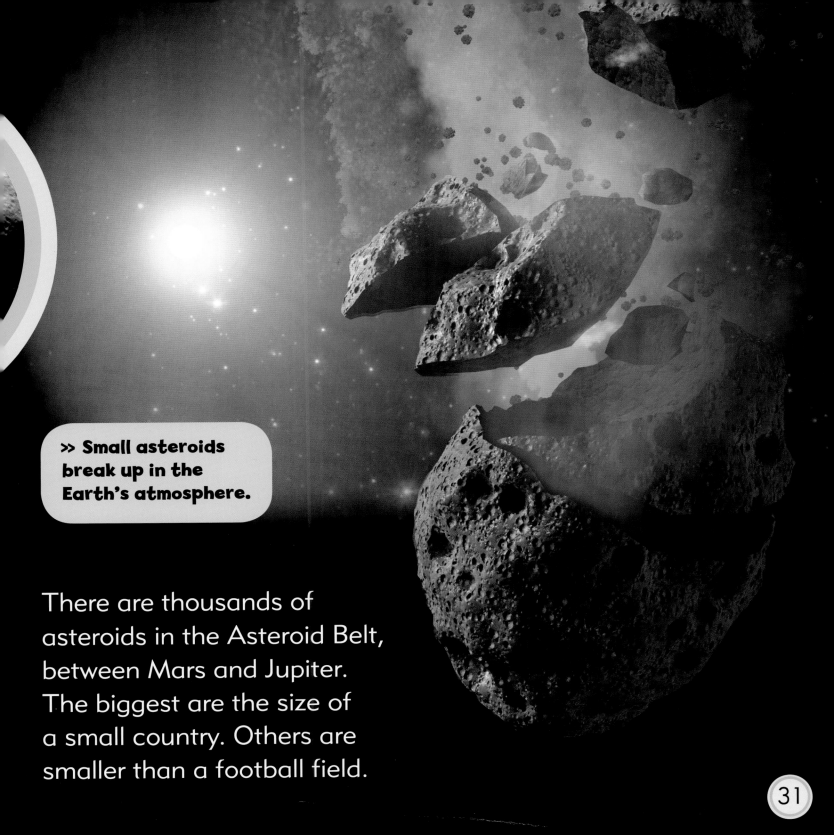

>> Small asteroids break up in the Earth's atmosphere.

There are thousands of asteroids in the Asteroid Belt, between Mars and Jupiter. The biggest are the size of a small country. Others are smaller than a football field.

Meteorites

Meteorites are lumps of rock or iron that have fallen to the Earth.

>> **Shooting stars, or meteors, are bright trails of light in the night sky.**

<< **The world's biggest meteorite lies where it fell, in Namibia, Africa. It weighs nearly 60 tonnes.**

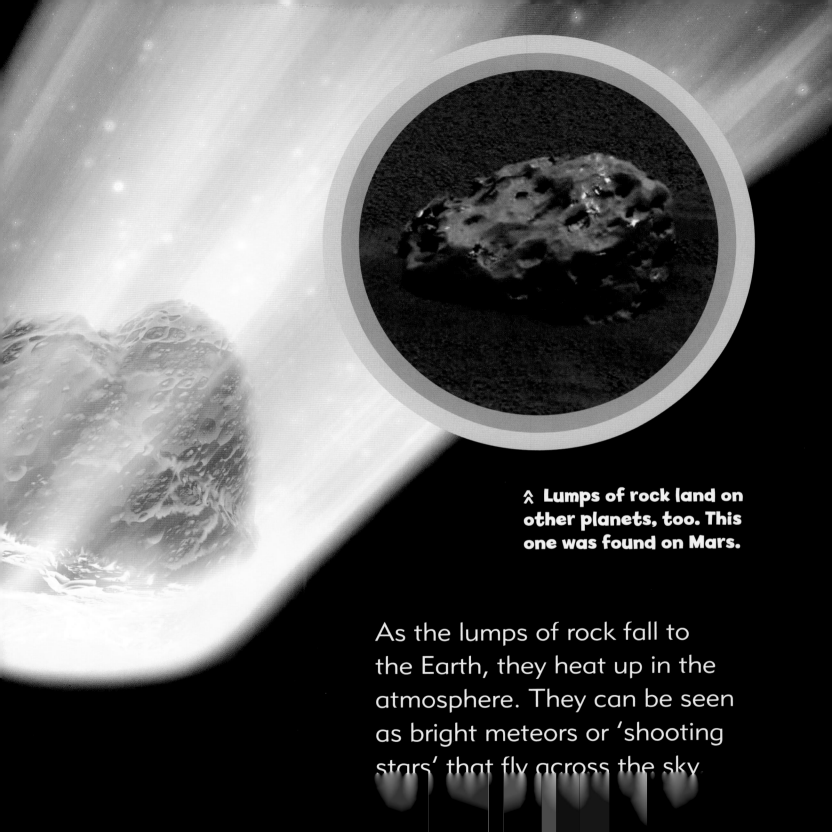

⌃ **Lumps of rock land on other planets, too. This one was found on Mars.**

As the lumps of rock fall to the Earth, they heat up in the atmosphere. They can be seen as bright meteors or 'shooting stars' that fly across the sky.

Stars

A star is a large ball of hot, burning gas. Stars shine by burning gas to make heat and light.

˅ **Many stars are found in groups, called clusters.**

Our Sun is the nearest star to the Earth. Other stars are so far away that they look like tiny dots of light and can only be seen at night.

« Our Sun is a medium-sized yellow star.

⌃ Stars come in different colours and sizes.

35

Life of a star

Like people, stars are born, grow old and die. Stars can live for billions of years.

>> Blue giants are large, hot stars that live short lives.

Blue giant

Yellow dwarf (the Sun)

Stars are born inside huge clouds of dust and gas. As they grow older they get bigger.

Most stars fade and cool when they run out of gas. But the biggest stars explode in a **supernova**.

↟ This cloud of gas and dust is full of newborn stars.

Constellations

Constellations are groups of stars that make patterns in the sky.

Southern Hemisphere

Northern Hemisphere

⌃ **Different constellations can be seen in the Northern and Southern Hemispheres.**

>> Orion can be seen here shining brightly in the night sky.

There are 88 constellations in the sky. Most of them are named after characters, creatures and objects from ancient legends.

>> Orion was named after a hunter. Three bright stars make his belt.

Galaxies

A galaxy is a massive group of stars, gas and dust moving through space.

⌄ **Sometimes galaxies crash into each other as they move through space.**

⌄ **Most galaxies are so far away that they can only be seen through a telescope.**

There are hundreds of billions of galaxies in the universe. They come in many shapes and sizes. Some belong to big groups of galaxies called clusters.

<< Spiral galaxies look like whirlpools.

The Milky Way

The Milky Way is the galaxy we live in. It is a flattened spiral shape.

⌄ **The Sun is located on one of the Milky Way's spiral arms.**

⌃ From the Earth, you can sometimes see a small part of the Milky Way.

⌃ The Milky Way is made up of hundreds of billions of stars.

Most of the stars in the Milky Way are so faint that they blend into a misty band. On a clear night, we can see this band stretching across the sky.

The universe

The universe contains everything we know about, from our home to the farthest, faintest galaxies in space.

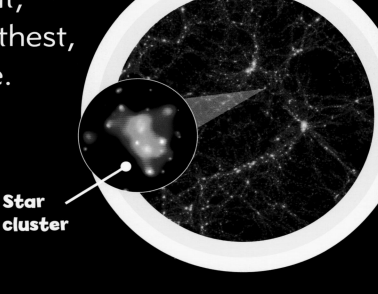

Star cluster

⌃ Clusters of galaxies make a spiderweb pattern in space.

⌃ This photo shows the faintest and most distant galaxies ever seen.

Astronomers think there are probably about 1000 billion galaxies in the universe. But no one knows how far it stretches, or what lies beyond it.

« Gas, dust and planets make up the parts of the universe that we can see.

The Big Bang

Astronomers think that the universe started with a sudden explosion, known as the Big Bang. This took place about 14 billion years ago.

>> The universe has kept growing ever since the Big Bang.

Everything in the universe started with a tiny, hot explosion. Over time, the universe has grown bigger and cooled down. Scientists think it is still growing.

>> **Special telescopes can detect** energy **from the Big Bang.**

Telescopes

Telescopes make distant objects appear closer. Astronomers use them to study space.

<< **Refracting telescopes use** lenses **to make an image appear larger.**

>> **Radio telescopes collect radio waves from far out in space and use them to create images.**

✣ **The Hubble Space Telescope is in orbit around the Earth.**

Some telescopes use lenses and mirrors to collect light and make an image. Others can see energy that is invisible to the eye, such as **radio waves** and **x-rays**.

Rockets

Rockets are used to launch spacecraft from the Earth's surface, through the atmosphere and into space.

« The first rocket to reach space was the German V-2 rocket in 1942.

≪ The moment a rocket leaves the ground is called 'blast-off'.

⌃ Rockets are the only type of engine that can work in space.

Rockets fly when very hot gases are blasted from a hole at their base. The rocket moves upwards, away from the gases.

Satellites

Satellites orbit planets or stars. Some are natural, such as moons. Others are machines launched to orbit the Earth.

˅ **Thousands of man-made satellites orbit the Earth.**

⌃ **Russia's Sputnik 1 was the first satellite, launched in 1957.**

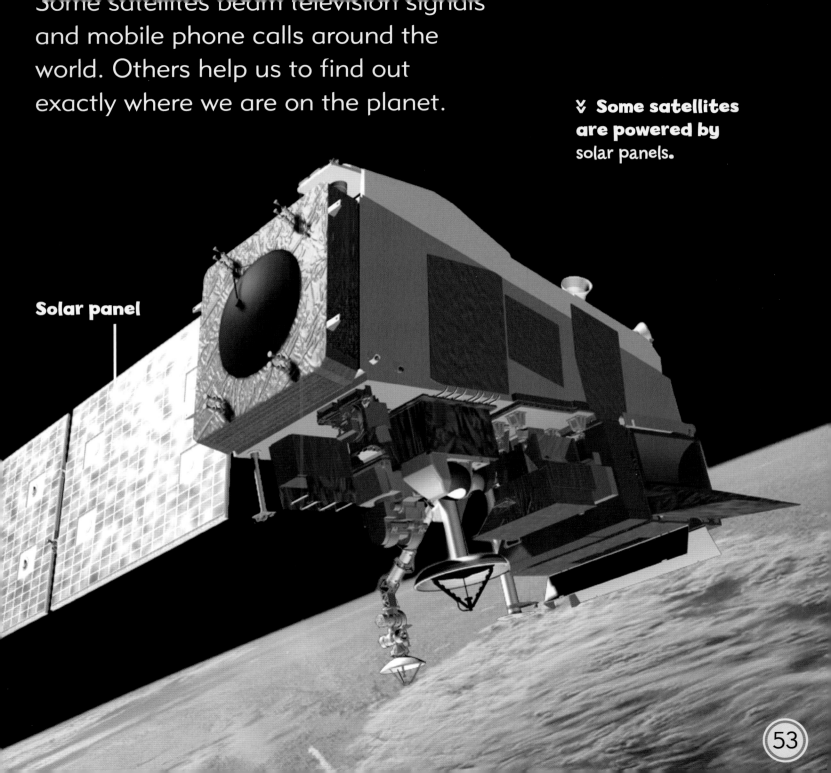

Some satellites beam television signals and mobile phone calls around the world. Others help us to find out exactly where we are on the planet.

⌄ **Some satellites are powered by** solar panels.

Solar panel

53

Astronauts

People who have been into space are called astronauts. Only a few hundred people have ever been into space.

∧ **Yuri Gagarin, the first astronaut, went into space in 1961.**

>> Astronauts must do lots of training before they go into space.

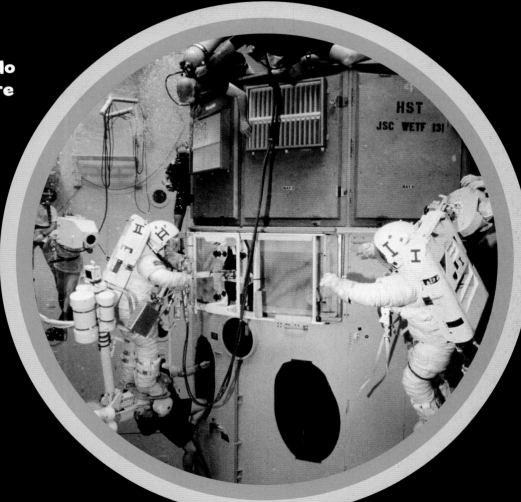

« Astronauts wear protective spacesuits to leave their spacecraft.

In space there is no **gravity** – the force that keeps you on the ground – so everything floats around. This makes simple tasks like washing your hair very difficult.

The first men on the Moon

On 20 July 1969, a spacecraft with people on board touched down on the Moon for the first time.

>> Buzz Aldrin (shown here) and Neil Armstrong were the first men to walk on the Moon.

<< **The Saturn V (Saturn Five) rocket launched the Apollo missions to the Moon.**

The landing was part of the United States' Apollo programme. A further five Apollo missions landed on the Moon.

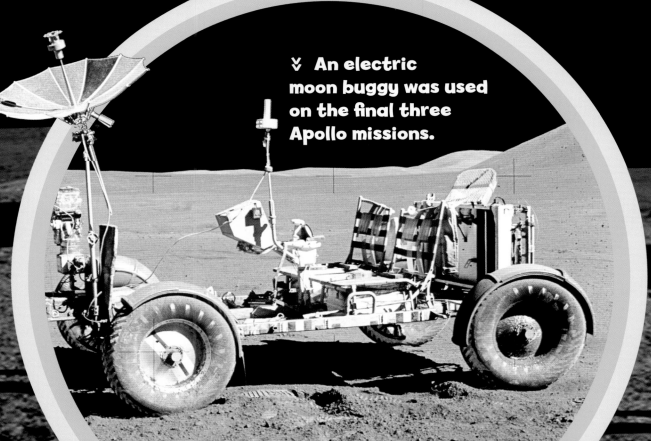

⌄ **An electric moon buggy was used on the final three Apollo missions.**

International Space Station

The International Space Station (ISS) is a science lab and **observatory** in orbit around the Earth.

⌃ **The bright streak seen here above the Moon shows the path taken by the ISS.**

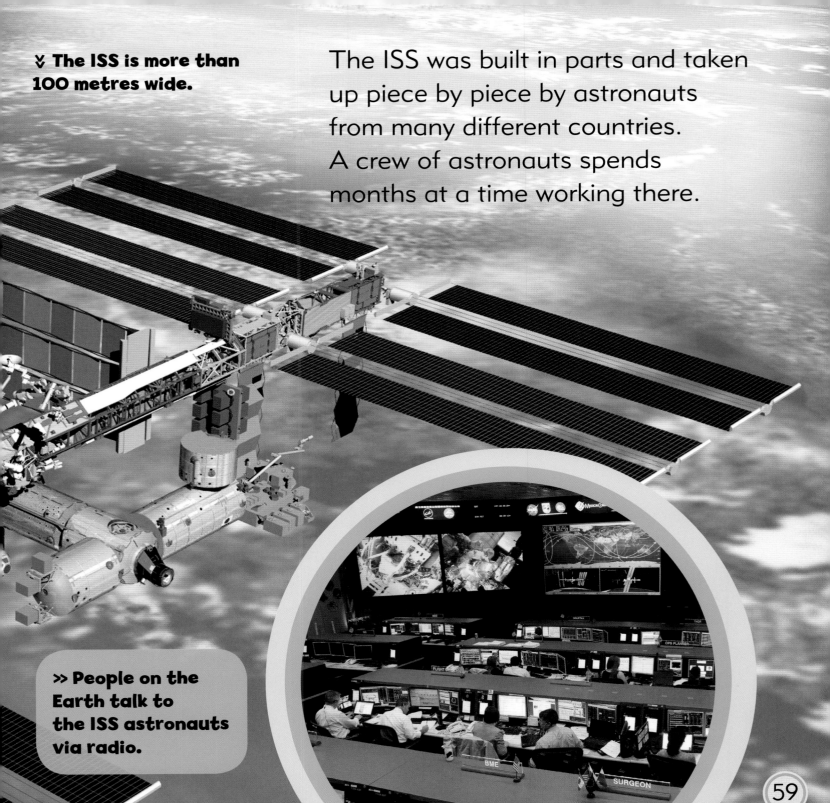

⌄ The ISS is more than 100 metres wide.

The ISS was built in parts and taken up piece by piece by astronauts from many different countries. A crew of astronauts spends months at a time working there.

>> People on the Earth talk to the ISS astronauts via radio.

Glossary

Atmosphere A layer of gas surrounding a planet.

Astronomer A scientist who studies objects in space.

Core The centre of a planet or star.

Crater A bowl-shaped dent in the surface of a moon or planet, made by a rock from space crashing into it.

Energy What is needed to power things. Heat, light and sound are types of energy.

Gas giant A huge planet with no solid surface. Jupiter, Saturn, Uranus and Neptune are all gas giants.

Gravity A force that pulls on objects.

Hemisphere Half a sphere. Planets are divided into northern and southern hemispheres by an imaginary line around the planet.

Ice caps Thick sheets of ice found at the top and bottom of Earth and Mars.

Lava Melted rock that flows out of a volcano.

Lens A piece of specially-shaped and polished glass used in some telescopes to collect light.

Methane A gas found in the atmospheres and lakes of some planets and moons.

Meteorite A space rock that lands on a planet or moon.

Observatory A building that is home to a telescope.

Orbit The path in space taken by one object around another, such as the Moon around the Earth.

Radio waves A type of energy given off by certain objects in space.

Solar panels Special flat boards often used by satellites to turn the Sun's energy into electricity.

Supernova The explosive death of an old, large star when it runs out of fuel.

X-ray A type of energy given off by certain objects in space.

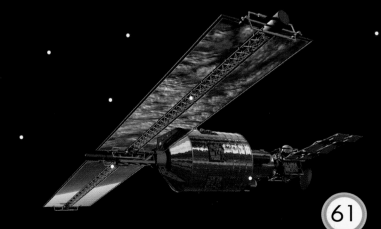

Index

Picture credits

Alamy

40bl © Horizons WWP, 46 © BSIP SA

Corbis

22-23 © William Radcliffe/Science Faction, 32bl © Radius Images

Getty Images

8l Stocktrek Images, 15tr David Nunuk, 16bl Stocktrek Images, 16-17 Stocktrek Images, 28bl UIG via Getty Images, 34bl Getty Images, 38 l&c SSPL via Getty Images, 39 (circle) Image Work/amanaimagesRF, 58l Babak Tafreshi, Twan

NASA

fc NASA/JHUAPL/Carnegie Institution of Washington image; ESA/Herschel/PACS/SPIRE/Hill, Motte; HOBYS Key Programme Consortium; U.S. Geological Survey / NASA; NASA/JPL/University of Arizona. bc NASA, 1 fl NASA Planetary Photojournal, 1tl NASA, 1c NASA, 1r NASA/JPL/Space Science Institute, 1b NASA, 2-3 NASA Tony Landis, 4-5 NASA, 6-7 Courtesy NASA/ JPL-Caltech, 8l (middlle image) NASA / JHU Applied Physics Lab / Carnegie Inst. Washington, 8-9 NASA / JHU Applied Physics Lab / Carnegie Inst. Washington, 9br NASA, 10bl NASA, 11 NASA/JPL/USGS, 14bl NASA, 14-15 NASA/JPL, 17tr NASA/JPL-Caltech, 18l NASA Planetary Photojournal, 18-19 NASA/JPL/University of Arizona, 19r NASA, 20tr NASA/JPL, Steven Hobbs (Brisbane, Queensland, Australia), 20-21 NASA/JPL/Space Science Institute, 21br NASA/JPL/University of Colorado, 22bl NASA, 23tr NASA/JPL/USGS, 24bl NASA Planetary Photojournal, 24-25 NASA Planetary Photojournal, 26bl NASA, ESA, JPL, and A. Feild (STScI), 30tr NASA/Johns Hopkins Applied Physics Laboratory, 31 NASA/JPL-Caltech, 33tr NASA/JPL/Cornell, 36-37 NASA/JPL-Caltech/UCLA, 37tr NASA/Walt Feimer, 41b NASA/JPL-Caltech/ESA/Harvard-Smithsonian CfA, 42bl NASA/ European Space Agency, 42-43 NASA JPL, 44l NASA; ESA; G. Illingworth, D. Magee, and P. Oesch, University of California, Santa Cruz; R. Bouwens, Leiden University; and the HUDF09 Team, 44r Virgo consortium; Reference: Jenkins et al. 1998, 45 NASA/ESA/Hubble Heritage Team, 47 NASA, 48bl Courtesy J. O'Leary (Maryland Science Center), 48-49 NASA, 49tr CSIRO/ Shaun Amy, 50bl NASA, 50-51 NASA, 52bl European Space Agency, 52tr NASA, 53 Ball Aerospace & Technologies Corp. NOAA JPSS-1 Satellite, 54l NASA, 54-55 NASA, 56-57 NASA, 57tl NASA, 57b NASA, 58-59 NASA, 59b NASA

Science Photo Library

1bl Chris Butler, 25tr David Hardy, 26-27 Chris Butler, 27br Lynette Cook, 28tr Royal Greenwich Observatory, 32-33 Michael Dunning, 34-35 (background) Lynette Cook, 39 (background) Babak Tafreshi, Twan, 40-41 NASA/ESA/STSCI/Hubble Heritage Team, 47 Detlev Van Ravenswaay, 51tr NASA/Science Photo Library, 55tr NASA

Shutterstock

fc dezignor, bc Vladimir Arndt, 6bl Linda Brotkorb, 7br Pakhnyushcha and Steshkin Yevgeniy, 10tr Dreamframer, 12-13 Andrea Danti, 13t Michelangelus, 13 (inset) Sebikus, 13b MarcelClemens, 29 Molodec, 30bl Andrea Danti, 34-35 (circle inset) Pavelk, 43tr Kevin Key, 46-47 (background) Igor Zh., 60 AND Inc, 62 Dundanim, 64 Nerthuz

Other

36bl Paul Stansifer